DISCIPLINE A

D1485189

The ACAS advisory handbook

WITHDRAWN
FROM STOCK
Treloar College
R05697P2386

CONTENTS

INTRODUCTION

The ACAS Code *Disciplinary Practice and Procedures in Employment* published in 1977, provides guidance on good practice in disciplinary matters. The Code is reproduced for reference purposes in Appendix 1.

This booklet is intended to complement the Code by providing more practical guidance. It is however purely advisory and does not have the status of a Code of Practice. The advice it contains takes account of case law and the development of good practice since 1977 to help employers and employees handle matters of discipline, absence and sub-standard work. The guidance is presented as far as possible in self-contained sections which can be referred to as and when needed. There is a summary of key points at the beginning of each section.

The booklet contains examples of good practice and is designed to help employers and employees in all types and size of organisation. Each organisation must decide what procedures and practices best suit its own circumstances. Larger, more complex organisations, for example, may need more formal disciplinary procedures; in small firms a more simple and straightforward procedure may suffice. It is managements' responsibility to ensure that disciplinary practices and procedures are effective, fair, well-understood and consistently applied.

Proper procedures are an aid to good management and should not be viewed primarily as a means of imposing sanctions or as necessarily leading to dismissal. Where dismissal does occur employees with two or more years service may complain to an industrial tribunal if they believe they have been dismissed unfairly.[1] It is for the employer to show the reason for the dismissal and that it was justified. The tribunal will determine whether the dismissal was fair or unfair and will take into account size and administrative resources in deciding whether the employer acted reasonably or unreasonably. In addition an employee, irrespective of

1 Section 98 of the Employment Rights Act 1996 covers the general position relating to fairness of dismissal. The Court of Appeal decided in a judgement in July 1995 that the two-year qualifying period for the right to complain of unfair dismissal was discriminatory against women for a dismissal occurring in 1991. At the time of writing a decision is awaited, following an appeal to the House of Lords.

length of service, may have a claim in common law for breach of contract for wrongful dismissal. Such a claim may be pursued through an action for damages in the courts or, alternatively, through an industrial tribunal if the employment has terminated.

1

CHECKLIST FOR HANDLING A DISCIPLINARY MATTER

This checklist sets out the key steps which employers should consider when handling a disciplinary matter. All employers, regardless of size, should observe the principles of natural justice embodied below:

1 Gather all the relevant facts:
- promptly before memories fade
- take statements, collect documents
- in serious cases consider suspension with pay while an investigation is conducted.

2 Be clear about the complaint:
- is action needed at this stage?

3 If so, decide whether the action should be:
- advice and counselling
- formal disciplinary action.

4 If formal action is required, arrange a disciplinary interview:
- ensure that the individual is aware of the nature of the complaint and that the interview is a disciplinary one
- tell the individual where and when the interview will take place and of a right to be accompanied.
- try to arrange for a second member of management to be present.

5 Start by introducing:
- those present and the purpose of the interview
- the nature of the complaint
- the supporting evidence.

6 Allow the individual to state his/her case:
- consider and question any explanations put forward.

7 If any new facts emerge:
- decide whether further investigation is required
- if it is, adjourn the interview and reconvene when the investigation is completed.

8 Except in very straightforward cases, call an adjournment before reaching a decision:
- come to a clear view about the facts
- if they are disputed, decide on the balance of probability what version of the facts is true.

9 Before deciding the penalty consider:
- the gravity of the offence and whether the procedure gives guidance
- the penalty applied in similar cases in the past
- the individual's disciplinary record and general service
- any mitigating circumstances
- whether the proposed penalty is reasonable in all the circumstances.

10 Reconvene the disciplinary interview to:
- clearly inform the individual of the decision and the penalty, if any
- explain the right of appeal and how it operates
- in the case of a warning, explain what improvement is expected, how long the warning will last and what the consequences of failure to improve may be.

11 Record the action taken:
- if other than an oral warning, confirm the disciplinary action to the individual in writing
- keep a simple record of the action taken for future reference.

12 Monitor the individual's performance:
- disciplinary action should be followed up with the object of encouraging improvement
- monitor progress regularly and discuss it with the individual.

Note: Examples of letters to use in disciplinary matters are given in Appendix 4.

2

THE NEED FOR RULES AND DISCIPLINARY PROCEDURES

Key Points:

Rules are necessary because they set standards. A good disciplinary procedure will help employees to keep to them and will help employers to deal fairly with those who do not.

Rules should normally cover issues such as absence, health and safety, misconduct, sub-standard performance, use of company facilities, timekeeping and holiday arrangements.

Rules and procedures should be clear and usually in writing and should be known and understood by all employees.

Every employee should have access to a copy of the rules and disciplinary procedure.

Management should aim to secure the involvement of employees and any recognised trade union or other employee representatives when disciplinary procedures are introduced or revised.

Rules should be reviewed from time to time.

Management should ensure that those responsible for operating disciplinary rules understand them and receive appropriate training.

Why have rules?

Clear rules benefit both employers and employees. They set standards of conduct at work and make clear to employees what is expected of them.

How should rules be drawn up and communicated?

☐ They should generally be written down to ensure that employees know what is required of them and to avoid misunderstanding

☐ Care should be taken to ensure that they are non-discriminatory and are applied irrespective of sex, marital status, racial group or disability[2]

☐ They should be readily available and managers should take all reasonable steps to ensure that all employees know and understand them

☐ An explanation of the rules should be given to all new employees when they join. Section 1 of the Employment Rights Act 1996 requires employers to provide employees with a written statement covering their main terms and conditions of employment. In addition, Section 3 of the Employment Rights Act 1996 requires employers with 20 or more employees to include in the written statement details of any disciplinary rules which are applicable

☐ Special attention should be paid to ensure that rules are understood by young people with little experience of working life and by employees whose English is limited

☐ Where a rule has fallen into disuse or has not been applied consistently, employees should always be told before there is any change in practice, and they should be issued with a revised written statement within one month of the change.

What should rules cover?

The following are examples of the kinds of issues which rules should cover. An example of the sort of rules which might be appropriate in a small company is given in Appendix 2.

2 The Equal Opportunities Commission and the Commission for Racial Equality have both produced Codes of Practice on avoidance of discriminatory practices or procedures. The Department for Education and Employment has published a Code of Practice on the employment of disabled people under the Disability Discrimination Act 1995 (available from the Stationery Office). The Race Relations Employment Advisory Service (RREAS) of the Department for Education and Employment can give help and advice and may be contacted at 14th Floor, Cumberland House, 200 Broad Street, Birmingham B15 1TA. Tel: 0121 244 8141/3.

Timekeeping:

- are employees required to 'clock-in'
- what rules apply to lateness?

Absence:

- who authorises absence
- who approves holidays
- who should employees notify when they are absent from work
- when should notification of absence take place
- when is a medical self-certificate sufficient
- when will a doctor's certificate be necessary?

Health and safety:

- are there special requirements regarding personal appearance or cleanliness eg. length of hair, jewellery, protective clothing
- are there special hazards
- are there non-smoking areas
- is alchohol prohibited?

Gross misconduct:[3]

- are the kind of offences regarded as gross misconduct and which could lead to dismissal without notice clearly specified?

Use of company facilities:

- are private telephone calls permitted
- are employees allowed to be on company premises outside working hours
- is company equipment generally available for personal use?

Discrimination:

- is it clear that racial and sexual abuse or harassment will be treated as disciplinary offences
- is there a rule about clothing or uniform which is disproportionately disadvantageous to a racial group and which cannot be justified on non-racial grounds
- is there a rule requiring higher language standards than are needed for safe and effective performance of the job
- is there a requirement about mobility of employment which cannot be justified on operational grounds and is disadvantageous to one sex?

3 An explanation of gross misconduct is given in Section 6 on page 29.

It is helpful if rules are written down so that both managers and employees are clearly aware what is expected of them. The rules should be made clear to any new employees and ideally they should be given their own copy. In the small firm it may be sufficient for rules to be displayed in a prominent place. In large firms it is good practice to include a section on rules in the company handbook and to discuss them during the induction programme.

Employees will more readily accept rules if care is taken to explain why they are necessary. They should be presented as giving information rather than as warnings; for example.....'For reasons of safety and security, you may not bring visitors on to company premises without the express permission of your manager.'

Unless there are valid reasons why different sets of rules should apply to different groups of workers - perhaps for health and safety reasons - rules should generally apply to all employees, be they management or shop-floor, full-time or part-time.

Why have a disciplinary procedure?

A disciplinary procedure is the means by which rules are observed and standards are maintained. It provides a method of dealing with any shortcomings in conduct or performance and can help an undisciplined or poorly performing employee to become effective again. The consistent application of a fair and effective disciplinary procedure will help to minimise disagreements about disciplinary matters and reduce the need for dismissals.

What should disciplinary procedures contain?

Paragraph 10 of the *Code of Practice* reproduced below recommends what disciplinary procedures should contain:

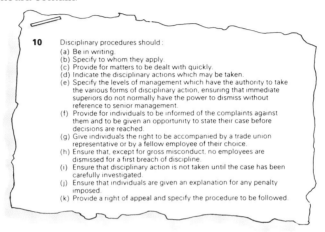

10   Disciplinary procedures should :
(a) Be in writing.
(b) Specify to whom they apply.
(c) Provide for matters to be dealt with quickly.
(d) Indicate the disciplinary actions which may be taken.
(e) Specify the levels of management which have the authority to take the various forms of disciplinary action, ensuring that immediate superiors do not normally have the power to dismiss without reference to senior management.
(f) Provide for individuals to be informed of the complaints against them and to be given an opportunity to state their case before decisions are reached.
(g) Give individuals the right to be accompanied by a trade union representative or by a fellow employee of their choice.
(h) Ensure that, except for gross misconduct, no employees are dismissed for a first breach of discipline.
(i) Ensure that disciplinary action is not taken until the case has been carefully investigated.
(j) Ensure that individuals are given an explanation for any penalty imposed.
(k) Provide a right of appeal and specify the procedure to be followed.

In addition, disciplinary procedures should:

apply to all employees, irrespective of their length of service

be non-discriminatory and applied irrespective of sex, marital status, race or disability

ensure that any investigatory period of suspension is with pay and specify how pay is to be calculated during such period (if, exceptionally, suspension is to be without pay, this should be provided for in the contract of employment)

ensure that, where the facts are in dispute, no disciplinary penalty is imposed until the case has been carefully investigated and it is concluded on the balance of probability that the employee committed the act in question.

Two examples of a disciplinary procedure are shown in Appendix 3. The first can be used by an organisation with formal relations with trade union(s) but the second example may be better suited to the needs of smaller firms.

Training

Those responsible for applying disciplinary rules and procedures should be trained for the task. If the provisions of an agreed disciplinary procedure are ignored when dismissing an employee, then this in itself is likely to have a bearing on the outcome of any subsequent complaint of unfair dismissal. Senior management should ensure that, wherever practicable, managers and supervisors have a thorough knowledge of their disciplinary rules and procedures and that they know how to prepare for and conduct a disciplinary interview. Where unions are recognised, consideration might be given to training managers and trade union representatives jointly.

2

3

HANDLING A DISCIPLINARY MATTER

Key Points:

Remember that disciplinary action is intended to encourage an unsatisfactory employee to improve.

Handle the matter promptly and gather all the relevant facts.

Be firm, it is a manager's responsibility to maintain satisfactory standards.

Consider suspension with pay while the case is investigated.

Be objective, fair and consistent.

Consider each case on its merits and avoid snap decisions made in the heat of the moment.

Follow the disciplinary procedure.

Encourage improvement

The main purpose of the disciplinary procedure is to encourage an employee whose standard of work or conduct is unsatisfactory to improve.

Handle promptly

Problems dealt with early enough can be 'nipped in the bud', whereas delay can make things worse. In all cases interviews should be arranged as soon as possible.

Gather facts

The manager should find out all the relevant facts promptly before memory fades, including anything the employee wishes to say. If in serious disciplinary cases there are witnesses, statements should be obtained from them at the earliest opportunity. The manager should be clear precisely what the complaint is. Personal details such as age, length of service, past disciplinary history and any current warnings should be obtained before the hearing as well as any necessary records or relevant documents.

Be firm .

The disciplinary procedure is there to provide a fair and consistent method of dealing with problems of conduct or work performance. Maintaining satisfactory standards and dealing with disciplinary issues requires firmness on the part of the manager.

Suspension with pay

In cases which appear to involve serious misconduct, a brief period of suspension should be considered while the case is being investigated. This should be with pay unless the contract of employment provides for suspension without pay in such circumstances. A suspension without pay should be exceptional as this in itself may amount to a disciplinary penalty. Where there has been physical violence, or where tempers have been raised, it is often wise to get those concerned off the premises as quickly as possible while the matter is investigated. They should be told clearly that they are suspended, that it will be for as short a period as possible and that they will be called back for interview.

3

Stay calm

Enquiries and proceedings should always be conducted with thought and care. Snap decisions made in the heat of the moment should be avoided. The disciplining of an employee is a serious matter and should never be regarded lightly or dealt with casually.

Be fair

Maintaining standards of acceptable conduct and work performance calls for objectivity and fairness. It is important to keep an open mind and not prejudge the issues.

Be consistent

The attitude and conduct of employees who obey rules will be seriously affected if management fails to apply the same rules and considerations to each case. Management should try to ensure that all employees are aware of the normal company practice for dealing with the misconduct or poor performance under consideration.

Consider each case on its merits

While consistency is important, it is essential to take account of the situations and people involved. Any decision to discipline an employee must be reasonable in all the circumstances.

Follow the disciplinary procedure

The disciplinary procedure should be followed and the supervisor or manager should never exceed the limits of his or her authority.

Is disciplinary action necessary?

Having gathered all the facts the manager or supervisor should decide whether to:

Drop the matter. There may be no case to answer or the matter may be so trivial that it is better to overlook it

Arrange counselling. This is an attempt to correct a situation and prevent it from getting worse without using the disciplinary procedure

Arrange a disciplinary interview. This will be necessary when the matter is more serious and it appears that there has been a disciplinary offence which requires appropriate disciplinary action.

3

4

COUNSELLING

Key Points:

Counselling may often be a more satisfactory method of resolving problems than a disciplinary interview.

It should take the form of a discussion with the objective of encouraging and helping the employee to improve.

The employee should fully understand the outcome.

A note of any counselling should be kept for reference purposes.

What is counselling?

In many cases the right word, at the right time and in the right way may be all that is needed and will often be a more satisfactory method of dealing with a breach of discipline than a formal interview.

How should it be done?

☐ Wherever possible hold the discussion out of the hearing of other employees. It should be a two-way discussion, aimed at pointing out any shortcomings in conduct or performance and encouraging improvement. Criticism should be constructive, and the emphasis should be on finding ways in which the employee can remedy any shortcomings

☐ Listen to any explanation put forward by the employee. If it becomes evident that there is no case to answer this should be made clear to the employee

☐ Where an improvement is required make sure that the employee understands what needs to be done, how performance or conduct will be reviewed, and over what period. The employee should be told that if there is no improvement the next stage will be the formal disciplinary procedure

☐ Take care that a counselling interview does not turn into a formal disciplinary hearing as this may unintentionally deny the employee certain rights, such as the right to be accompanied. If during the meeting it becomes obvious that the matter is more serious, the discussion should be adjourned. It should be made clear that the matter will be pursued under the formal disciplinary procedure

☐ Keep a brief note of any counselling for reference purposes. It should not be confused with action taken under the formal disciplinary procedure.

4

5

HOLDING A DISCIPLINARY INTERVIEW

Key Points:

Prepare for a disciplinary interview carefully and ensure all the relevant facts are available.

Tell the employee what is being alleged and advise him or her of any rights under the disciplinary procedure.

Give the employee time to prepare and an opportunity to state his or her case.

Carry out sufficient investigation and come to a clear view about the facts.

Consider adjourning the hearing before deciding on any disciplinary penalty to allow proper consideration of all the matters raised.

Preparing for the interview

- [ ] Prepare carefully and ensure you have all the facts
- [ ] Tell the employee of the complaint, the procedure to be followed and that he or she is required to attend a disciplinary interview
- [ ] Tell the employee that he or she is entitled to be accompanied at the interview
- [ ] Find out if there are any special circumstances to be taken into account. (For example, are there personal or other outside issues affecting performance or conduct?)
- [ ] Exercise care when dealing with evidence provided by an informant who wishes to remain anonymous. Take written statements, seek corroborative evidence and check that the informant's motives are genuine
- [ ] Are the standards of other employees acceptable or is this employee being unfairly singled out?
- [ ] Consider what explanations may be offered by the employee and, if possible. check them out beforehand
- [ ] Allow the employee time to prepare his or her case. In complex cases it may be useful and save time at the interview if copies of any relevant papers are given to the employee in advance
- [ ] If the employee concerned is a trade union official ensure that no disciplinary action beyond an oral warning is taken until the circumstances of the case have been discussed with a trade union representative or full-time official. This is because the action may be seen as an attack on the union's function
- [ ] Arrange a time and, if possible, a quiet place for the interview with adequate seating, where there will be no interruptions
- [ ] Ensure that all the relevant facts are available, such as personal details, disciplinary record and any current warnings, other relevant documents (eg. absence or sickness records) and, where appropriate, written statements from witnesses
- [ ] Establish what disciplinary action was taken in similar circumstances in the past
- [ ] Where possible arrange for a second member of management to be present to take notes of the

5

proceedings and to act as a witness, particularly if the employee is to be accompanied

☐ Where possible ensure that any witnesses who can do so attend the interview, unless the employee accepts in advance that the witness statements are statements of fact

☐ If the witness is someone from outside the company who is not prepared to attend the interview, try to get a written statement from him or her

☐ If there are likely to be language difficulties consider whether a friend of the employee can assist as an interpreter or other arrangements can be made

☐ Consider how the interview will be structured and make notes of the points which need to be covered.

How should a disciplinary interview be conducted?

Interviews rarely proceed in neat, orderly stages but the following guidelines should help:

introduce those present to the employee and explain why they are there

explain that the purpose of the interview is to consider whether disciplinary action should be taken in accordance with the company's disciplinary procedure

explain how the interview will be conducted.

Statement of the complaint

state precisely what the complaint is and outline the case briefly by going through the evidence that has been gathered. Ensure that the employee and his or her representative is allowed to see any statements made by witnesses or is told very clearly exactly what they contain

remember that the object of the interview is to discover the truth, not to catch people out. Establish whether the employee is prepared to accept that he or she has done something wrong. Then agree the steps which should be taken to remedy the situation.

Employee's reply

give the employee the opportunity to state his or her case, ask questions, present evidence and call witnesses. Listen attentively and be sensitive to silence as this can be a constructive way of

encouraging the employee to be more forthcoming
if it is not practical for witnesses to attend, consider
proceeding if it is clear that their evidence will not
affect the substance of the complaint.

General questioning and discussion

use this stage to establish all the facts

adjourn the interview if further investigation is
necessary or, if appropriate, at the request of the
employee's representative

ask the employee if he or she has any explanation for
the misconduct or failure to improve or if there are
any special circumstances to be taken into account

if it becomes clear during this stage that the
employee has provided an adequate explanation or
there is no real evidence to support the allegation,
stop the proceedings

keep the approach formal and polite but encourage
the employee to talk freely with a view to
establishing all the facts. A properly conducted
disciplinary interview should be a two-way process.
Use questions to clarify all the issues and to check
that what has been said is understood. Ask open-
ended questions (eg. What happened then?) to get
the broad picture. Ask precise, closed questions
requiring a yes/no answer only when specific
information is needed

try not to get involved in arguments and do not make
personal or humiliating remarks. Avoid physical
contact or gestures which the employee might
regard as threatening.

Summing up

After general questioning and discussion summarise
the main points concerning the offence, the main points
raised by the employee and any matters that need to
be checked. This will ensure that nothing has been
missed and will help demonstrate to the employee that
he or she has been given a fair hearing.

Adjournment

It is generally good practice to adjourn before a
decision is taken about a disciplinary penalty. This
allows proper consideration of all the matters raised.

Do any further checking that is necessary and come to
a clear view about what took place. Where the facts are

in dispute, decide which version is the most probable. If new facts emerge, consider whether the disciplinary interview needs to be reconvened.

What problems may arise and how should they be handled?

Not every disciplinary interview will go smoothly. Where problems are expected it is particularly important to ensure, wherever possible, that a second member of management and, where requested, an employee representative are present.

If the employee becomes emotionally distressed during the interview, allow time for the employee to become composed before continuing. The issues however cannot be avoided. If the employee continues to be so distressed that the interview cannot continue, it should be adjourned and resumed at a later date.

During the interview a certain amount of 'letting off steam' may be inevitable. This may be no bad thing and may be helpful in finding out and understanding precisely what happened. However, if misconduct or gross misconduct - for example abusive language or threatened physical violence - takes place during the interview treat it as such. Adjourn the interview and reconvene it at a later date when this offence can be considered as well. Consider suspending the employee with pay to allow time for him or her to calm down and to allow a full investigation.

5

6

DECIDING AND IMPLEMENTING DISCIPLINARY ACTION

Key Points:

Before deciding whether a disciplinary penalty is appropriate consider the employee's disciplinary and general record, whether the disciplinary procedure points to the likely penalty, action taken in previous cases, any explanations and circumstances to be considered and whether the penalty is reasonable.

Dismissal for gross misconduct without warnings or notice should only be for very serious offences (examples of which should be specified in the rules) and should only occur after a normal disciplinary investigation and interview.

Leave the employee in no doubt as to the nature of the disciplinary penalty, the improvement expected and the method of appeal.

Except in the event of an oral warning, give the employee written details of any disciplinary action.

Keep records of disciplinary action secure and confidential.

Do not normally allow disciplinary action to count against an employee indefinitely.

What should be considered before deciding any disciplinary penalty?

When deciding whether a disciplinary penalty is appropriate and what form it should take, consideration should be given to:

- whether the disciplinary procedure indicates what the likely penalty will be as a result of the particular misconduct
- the penalty imposed in similar cases in the past
- any special circumstances which might make it appropriate to lessen the severity of the penalty
- the employee's disciplinary record, general record, age, position, and length of service
- whether the proposed penalty is reasonable in view of all the circumstances.

It should be clear what the normal company practice is for dealing with the kind of misconduct or poor performance under consideration. This does not mean that similar offences will always call for similar disciplinary action: each case must be looked at on its merits and any relevant circumstances taken into account. These may include health or domestic problems, provocation, ignorance of the rule or standard involved or inconsistent treatment in the past.

If there is doubt about what disciplinary action to take, consider consulting other managers or the personnel department if there is one. If guidance is needed on formal disciplinary action seek advice, where possible, from someone who will not be involved in hearing any potential appeal.

Imposing the disciplinary penalty

- [ ] In the case of minor offences, the individual should be given a formal oral warning and told that a note that it was given will be kept for reference purposes
- [ ] In the case of more serious offences or where there is an accumulation of minor offences the individual should be given a formal written warning
- [ ] If the employee has received a previous warning, further misconduct may warrant a final written warning or consideration of a disciplinary penalty

short of dismissal (including disciplinary transfer, disciplinary suspension without pay,[4] demotion, loss of seniority, or loss of increment provided these penalties are allowed for by an express or implied term of the contract of employment)

- [ ] There may be occasions when misconduct is considered not to be so serious as to justify dismissal but serious enough to warrant only one written warning which will be both the first and final
- [ ] A final written warning should contain a statement that any further misconduct will lead to dismissal
- [ ] If all previous stages have been observed, the final step will be dismissal.

It will be seen that a three stage procedure is recommended before dismissal namely: formal oral warning, first written warning, and final written warning. This does not however mean that three warnings must always be given before any dismissal is considered. There may be occasions when, depending on the seriousness of the misconduct involved, it will be appropriate to enter the procedure at stage 2 (written warning) or stage 3 (final written warning). There also may be occasions when dismissal without notice is applicable (see below).

Dismissal with notice

Dismissal should be the final step and only taken if, despite warnings, conduct or performance does not improve. It must be reasonable in all the circumstances of the case.

Unless the employee is being dismissed for reasons of gross misconduct (see below), he or she should receive the appropriate period of notice or payment in lieu of notice. This should include payments to cover the value of any fringe benefits such as use of company car, medical insurance, subsidised meals and any commission which the employee might otherwise have earned. Minimum periods of notice are laid down by law. Employees are entitled to at least one week's notice if they have worked for a month but less than two years. This increases by one week (up to a maximum of 12) for each completed year of service. If the contract of employment gives rights to more notice than the statutory minima, then the longer period of notice applies.[5]

4 Special consideration should be given before imposing disciplinary suspension without pay. Where it is imposed, it should not exceed any period indicated in the contract nor be unreasonably prolonged since it would then be open to the employee to take action for breach of contract or resign and claim constructive dismissal.

5 Further guidance on employees' rights to notice is provided in the Department of Trade and Industry's booklet: *Rights to notice and reasons for dismissal*, Employment Legislation Booklet PL 707, which is available free from most Jobcentres.

Dismissal without notice

Employers should give all employees a clear indication of the type of misconduct which, in the light of the requirements of the employer's business, will warrant dismissal without the normal period of notice or pay in lieu of notice. So far as possible the types of offence which fall into this category (gross misconduct) should be clearly specified in the rules.

A dismissal for gross misconduct should only take place after the normal investigation to establish all the facts. The employee should be told of the complaint and be given an opportunity to state his or her case and be represented.

Gross misconduct is generally seen as misconduct serious enough to destroy the employment contract between the employer and the employee and make any further working relationship and trust impossible. It is normally restricted to very serious offences - for example physical violence, theft or fraud - but may be determined by the nature of the business or other circumstances.

How should an employee be informed of the disciplinary decision?

The employee should be informed orally of the decision in all cases. If further investigations have taken place during the adjournment the employee should be told about the result of these before announcing the decision. The reasons for the decision should be given and the employee left in no doubt as to what action is being taken under the disciplinary procedure. If, for example, an oral warning is being given it should be made clear to the employee that this is not just a reprimand. The period of time that any warning will remain in force should also be explained. The employee should be told clearly what improvement is required, over what period and how it will be assessed.

Written notification of disciplinary action

Except in the event of an oral warning, details of any disciplinary penalty should be given in writing to the employee. A copy should be retained by the employer. The written notification should specify:

- the nature of the misconduct
- any period of time given for improvement and the improvement expected
- the disciplinary penalty and, where appropriate, how long it will last
- the likely consequences of further misconduct
- the timescale for lodging an appeal and how it should be made.

Written reasons for dismissal

Employees with two years' service have a right to request a 'written statement of reasons for dismissal'. Employers are required by law to comply within 14 days of the request being made, unless it is not reasonably practicable. A woman who is dismissed during pregnancy or maternity leave is automatically entitled to the written statement without having to request it and irrespective of length of service.[6] The written statement can be used in evidence in any subsequent proceedings, for example in relation to a complaint of unfair dismissal.

6 Section 92 of the Employment Right Act 1996 refers. Fuller details of employees' rights written reasons for dismissal are given in the Department Trade and Industry free booklet *Rights notice and reasons for dismissal* (PL70

What records should be kept?

Consistent handling of disciplinary matters will be impracticable unless simple records of earlier decisions are kept. These records should be confidential, detailing the nature of any breach of disciplinary rules, the action taken and the reasons for it, the date action was taken, whether an appeal was lodged, its outcome and any subsequent developments.

Time limits for warnings

Except in agreed special circumstances, any disciplinary action taken should be disregarded for disciplinary purposes after a specified period of satisfactory conduct. This period should be established clearly when the disciplinary procedure is being drawn up. Normal practice is for different periods for different types of warnings. In general, warnings for minor offences may be valid for up to 6 months, whilst final

6

warnings may remain in force for 12 months or more. Warnings should cease to be 'live' following the specified period of satisfactory conduct and should be disregarded for future disciplinary purposes. There may, however, be occasions where an employee's conduct is satisfactory throughout the period the warning is in force, only to lapse very soon thereafter. Where a pattern emerges and there is evidence of abuse, the employee's disciplinary record should be borne in mind in deciding how long any current warning should last.

Exceptionally, there may be circumstances where the misconduct is so serious - verging on gross misconduct - that it cannot realistically be disregarded for future disciplinary purposes. In such circumstances it should be made very clear that the final written warning can never be removed and that any recurrence will lead to dismissal.

6

7

HOLDING
AN APPEAL

Key Points:

Provide for appeals to be dealt with speedily.

Wherever possible, use a procedure which is separate from the general grievance procedure.

Wherever possible, provide for the appeal to be heard by an authority higher than that taking the disciplinary action.

Pay particular attention to any new evidence introduced at the hearing and allow the employee to comment on it.

Examine all the issues fully and do not be afraid to overturn a wrong decision.

What should an appeals procedure contain?

It should:

- [ ] Specify any time-limit within which the appeal should be lodged
- [ ] Provide for appeals to be dealt with speedily, particularly those involving suspension without pay or dismissal
- [ ] Wherever possible, provide for the appeal to be heard by an authority higher than that taking the disciplinary action
- [ ] Spell out the action which may be taken by those hearing the appeal
- [ ] Provide that the employee, or a representative if the employee so wishes, has an opportunity to comment on any new evidence arising during the appeal before any decision is taken.

Small firms

In small firms there may be no authority higher than the manager who decided the disciplinary action. If this is the case the same person who took the disciplinary action should hear the appeal and act as impartially as possible. The occasion should be seen as an opportunity to review the original decision in an objective manner and at a quieter time. This can be more readily achieved if some time is allowed to elapse before the appeal hearing.

How should an appeal hearing be conducted?

Action prior to the appeal

- [ ] Inform the employee of the arrangements for the appeal hearing and his or her rights under the procedure
- [ ] Ensure that the relevant records are available and study them prior to the appeal hearing.

The appeal hearing

- [ ] Introduce those present to the employee
- [ ] Explain the purpose of the hearing, how it will be conducted and what powers the appeal panel has
- [ ] Ask the employee why he or she is appealing against the disciplinary penalty

7

- [ ] Pay particular attention to any new evidence that has been introduced, and ensure the employee has the opportunity to comment on it
- [ ] Once all the relevant issues have been thoroughly explored, summarise the facts and call an adjournment to consider what decision to come to
- [ ] Do not be afraid to overturn a previous decision if it becomes apparent that this was not soundly based and do not regard such action as undermining authority. In practice it should help ensure that a correct decision is made next time[7]
- [ ] Inform the employee of the results of the appeal and the reasons for the decision and confirm it in writing. Make it clear, if it is the case, that the decision is final.

7 Discuss successful appeals with subordinate managers and explain the reasons. Consider whether further training is appropriate.

Industrial tribunal time limits

Subject to the satisfaction of certain conditions, employees who feel that they have been unfairly dismissed have a legal right to make a complaint of unfair dismissal to an industrial tribunal. Such complaints must normally be received by the tribunal within three months of the employee's last day of work.

In most cases decisions of an internal appeal procedure will be reached well within this three month period. In exceptional cases a decision may take longer than three months. Where this seems likely to happen employees should consider whether to present an application to the industrial tribunal and ask that the case is not set down for hearing until the outcome of the internal appeal is known. Employers should not regard this action as affecting the internal appeal in any way.

7

8

PARTICULAR CASES

Key Points:

Consider how disciplinary matters should be handled when management and union representatives are not immediately available.

In normal circumstances take no disciplinary action, beyond an oral warning, against a trade union official until the case has been discussed with a senior trade union representative or full-time official.

In criminal cases:

Do not dismiss or discipline an employee merely because he or she has been charged with or convicted of a criminal offence.

Decide whether the employee's conduct affects ability or suitability for continued employment. If it does, use normal disciplinary rules. If it does not, decide whether in the light of the needs of the business, the employee's job can be kept open throughout the period of absence.

Base any decision on a reasonable belief following a reasonable investigation into the circumstances of the case.

Where a criminal charge has been made, do not defer taking fair and reasonable disciplinary action, if appropriate, merely because the outcome of the prosecution is not known.

What types of case require particular consideration?

Paragraph 15 of the *Code of Practice* recommends that certain cases may need special consideration. Employers may find the following additional advice helpful, particularly in relation to alleged criminal offences.

Employees to whom the full procedure is not immediately available.

It may be sensible to allow time off with pay, so that employees who work in isolated locations or on shifts can attend a disciplinary interview on the main site during normal working hours. Alternatively, if a number of witnesses need to attend, it may be better to hold the disciplinary interview on the nightshift or at the particular location.

Trade union officials

Although normal disciplinary standards should apply to their conduct as employees, disciplinary action against a trade union official can be misconstrued as an attack on the union. Such problems can be avoided by early discussion with a full-time official.

Criminal offences

An employee should not be dismissed or otherwise disciplined merely because he or she has been charged with or convicted of a criminal offence. The question to be asked in such cases is whether the employee's conduct warrants action because of its employment implications.

Where it is thought that the conduct warrants disciplinary action, the following guidance should be borne in mind:

- [ ] The employer should investigate the facts as far as possible, come to a view about them and consider whether the conduct is sufficiently serious to warrant instituting the disciplinary procedure

- [ ] Where the conduct requires prompt attention, the employer need not await the outcome of the prosecution before taking fair and reasonable action

- [ ] Where the police are called in they should not be asked to conduct any investigation on behalf of the employer; nor should they be present at any disciplinary hearing or interview.

8

In some cases the nature of the alleged offence may not justify disciplinary action — for example, off-duty conduct which has no bearing on employment — but the employee may not be available for work because he or she is in custody or on remand. In these cases employers should decide whether, in the light of the needs of the business, the employee's job can be kept open. Where a criminal conviction leads, for example, to the loss of a licence so that continued employment in a particular job would be illegal, employers should consider whether suitable alternative work is available.

Where an employee, charged with or convicted of a criminal offence, refuses to co-operate with the employer's disciplinary investigations and proceedings, this should not deter an employer from taking action. The employee should be advised in writing that unless further information is provided, a disciplinary decision will be taken on the basis of the information available and could result in dismissal.

Where there is little likelihood of an employee returning to employment, it may be argued that the contract of employment has been terminated through 'frustration'.[8] The doctrine is normally accepted by the courts only where the frustrating event renders all performance of the employment contract clearly impossible.

An employee who has been charged with, or convicted of, a criminal offence may become unacceptable to colleagues, resulting in workforce pressure to dismiss and threats of industrial action. Employers should bear in mind that they may have to justify the reasonableness of any decision to dismiss and that an industrial tribunal will ignore threats of, and actual, industrial action when determining the fairness of a decision (Section 107, Employment Rights Act 1996). They should consider all relevant factors, not just disruption to production, before reaching a reasonable decision.

8 There are circumstances where operation of law terminates a contract of employment, in particular the 'doctrine of frustration', without a dismissal taking place. In law 'frustration' occurs when, without the fault of either party, some event, which was not reasonably foreseeable at the time of the contract, renders future performance either impossible or something radically different from what was contemplated originally. The doctrine is usually invoked in cases of sickness or imprisonment of the employee.

8

9

ABSENCE

Key Points:

Before any action is taken to dismiss an employee who is absent from work always:

carry out a full investigation into the reasons for the absence

give the employee an opportunity to state his or her case and be accompanied

issue warnings and give time for improvement where appropriate

consider whether suitable alternative employment is available

act reasonably in all the circumstances.

This section considers how to handle problems of absence and gives guidance about short-term and long-term absences.[9] A distinction should be made between absence on grounds of illness or injury and absence for reasons which may call for disciplinary action. Where disciplinary action is called for, the normal disciplinary procedure should be used. Where the employee is absent because of illness or injury the guidance in this section of the booklet should be followed.

Records showing lateness and the duration of and reasons for all spells of absence should be kept to help monitor absence levels. These enable management to check levels of absence or lateness so that problems can be spotted and addressed at an early stage.[10]

9 Further guidance on the subject of absence is given in the ACAS Advisory Booklet *Absence and Labour Turnover*.

10 Guidance on the subject of personnel records is given in the ACAS Advisory Booklet *Personnel Records*.

How should frequent and persistent short-term absence be handled?

☐ Absences should be investigated promptly and the employee asked to give an explanation

☐ Where there is no medical advice to support frequent self- certified absences, the employee should be asked to consult a doctor to establish whether medical treatment is necessary and whether the underlying reason for absence is work-related

☐ If after investigation it appears that there were no good reasons for the absences, the matter should be dealt with under the disciplinary procedure

☐ Where absences arise from temporary domestic problems, the employer in deciding appropriate action should consider whether an improvement in attendance is likely

☐ In all cases the employee should be told what improvement in attendance is expected and warned of the likely consequences if this does not happen

☐ If there is no improvement, the employee's age, length of service, performance, the likelihood of a change in attendance, the availability of suitable alternative work and the effect of past and future absences on the business should all be taken into account in deciding appropriate action.

9

It is essential that persistent absence is dealt with promptly, firmly and consistently in order to show both the employee concerned and other employees that absence is regarded as a serious matter and may result in dismissal. An examination of records will identify those employees who are regularly absent and may show an absence pattern. In such cases employers should make sufficient enquiries to determine whether the absence is because of genuine illness or for other reasons.

How should longer-term absence through ill-health be handled?

☐ The employee should be contacted periodically and in turn should maintain regular contact with the employer

☐ The employee should be kept fully informed if employment is at risk

☐ Before applying to an employee's doctor for a medical report, the employer must notify the employee in writing that it is proposed to make the application and secure the employee's consent in writing.[11]

☐ In addition the employer must inform the individual that he or she has:

the right to withhold consent to the application being made

the right to state that he or she wishes to have access to the report (The Act also gives an individual the right to have access to the medical practitioner's report for up to six months after it was supplied)

rights concerning access to the report before (or after) it is supplied

the right to withhold consent to the report being supplied to the employer and

the right to request amendments to the report

☐ Where an employee states that he or she wishes to have access to the report, the employer must let the GP know this when making the application and at the same time let the employee know that the report has been requested

☐ The letter of enquiry reproduced in Appendix 4 (vii), and approved by the British Medical Association, may be used and the employee's

[11] Access to Medical Reports Act 1988.

permission to the enquiry should be attached to the letter.[12]

☐ The employee must contact the GP within 21 days of the date of application to make arrangements to see the report. Otherwise, the rights under the Act will be lost

☐ If the employee considers the report to be incorrect or misleading, the employee may make a written request to the GP to make appropriate amendments

☐ If the GP refuses, the employee has the right to ask the GP to attach a statement to the report reflecting the employee's view on any matters of disagreement

☐ The employee may withhold consent to the report being supplied to the employer

☐ On the basis of the GP's report the employer should consider whether alternative work is available

☐ The employer is not expected to create a special job for the employee concerned, nor to be a medical expert, but to take action on the basis of the medical evidence

☐ Where there is reasonable doubt about the nature of the illness or injury, the employee should be asked if he or she would agree to be examined by a doctor to be appointed by the company

☐ Where an employee refuses to co-operate in providing medical evidence or to undergo an independent medical examination, the employee should be told in writing that a decision will be taken on the basis of the information available and that it could result in dismissal

☐ Where the employee is allergic to a product used in the workplace, the employer should consider remedial action or a transfer to alternative work

☐ Where the employee's job can no longer be kept open and no suitable alternative work is available, the employee should be informed of the likelihood of dismissal

☐ Where dismissal action is taken, the employee should be given the period of notice to which he or she is entitled and informed of any right of appeal.

Where an employee has been on long-term sick absence and there is little likelihood of he or she becoming fit enough to return, it may be argued that the

12 The GP should return the report via the company doctor. If there is not one, the employer should make it clear to the employee, when seeking permission to approach the GP, that the report will be sent to the employer direct. Employers who wish to seek advice on securing the services of a company doctor should contact the Faculty of Occupational Medicine at 6 St Andrews Place, Regents Park, London NW1 4LB. Tel: 0171 387 4499.

contract of employment has been terminated through 'frustration'. (See Section 8 on particular cases). However, the doctrine of frustration should not be relied upon since the courts are generally reluctant to apply it where a procedure exists for termination of the contract. It is therefore better for the employer to take dismissal action

Where it is decided to dismiss an employee who has been on long-term sick absence, the normal conditions for giving notice will apply, even though in practice the employee will be unable to work the notice. In such circumstances, the employee should receive wages throughout the notice period or wages in lieu of notice as a lump sum.

Employees with special health problems

Consideration should be given to introducing measures to help employees, regardless of status or seniority, who are suffering from alcohol or drug abuse. The aim should be to identify employees affected and encourage them to seek help and treatment. There are a number of symptoms related to alcohol or drug abuse including poor performance, changes in personality, irritability, slurred speech, impaired concentration and memory, deterioration in personal hygiene, anxiety and depression. Where it is established that an employee is suffering from alcohol or drug abuse, employers should consider whether it is appropriate to treat the problem as a medical rather than a disciplinary matter. In all cases the employee should be encouraged to seek appropriate medical assistance. [13]

Where individuals suffer from, or are thought to suffer from, a medical condition making them unacceptable to work colleagues[14], there may sometimes be workforce pressure to dismiss or threats of industrial action. If an employee is dismissed, then he or she may be able to claim unfair dismissal before an industrial tribunal where the employer would have to justify the reasonableness of the decision. Also, the Disability Discrimination Act 1995 makes it unlawful for an employer with 20 or more employees to treat a disabled person less favourably for a reason relating to their disability, without a justifiable reason. Employers are required to make a reasonable adjustment to working conditions or the workplace where that would help to accommodate a particular disabled person.

13 In some areas there are specialist advice centres which can provide assistance.

14 HIV and AIDS
Current medical opinion indicates that there is no risk of becoming infected with HIV in most jobs. The virus is not transmitted through normal social or work interaction. The Health Education Authority, in its publication *HIV and AIDS at Work*, states that the risk of infection at work is negligible and there is no justification for discrimination against anyone with HIV infection or AIDS. This publication also gives guidelines to companies on how to develop a policy on HIV infection and AIDS. It should be noted that a person with HIV infection is covered by the Disability Discrimination Act when the condition leads to an impairment which has some effect on the ability to carry out normal day-to-day activities.

9

Failure to return from extended leave on the agreed date

Employers may have policies which allow employees extended leave of absence without pay, for example to visit relatives in their countries of origin or relatives who have emigrated to other countries, or to nurse a sick relative. There is no general statutory right to such leave without pay and whether it is granted is a matter for agreement between employers and their employees, or where appropriate, their trade unions.

Where a policy on extended leave is in operation, the following points should be borne in mind:

- [ ] The policy should apply to all employees, irrespective of their sex, marital status, racial group or disability

- [ ] Any conditions attaching to the granting of extended leave should be carefully explained to the employee and the employee's signature should be obtained as an acknowledgement that he or she understands and accepts them

- [ ] If an employee fails to return on the agreed date, this should be treated as any other failure to abide by the rules and circumstances should be investigated in the normal way as fully as possible

- [ ] Care should be taken to ensure that foreign medical certificates are not treated in a discriminatory way: employees can fall ill while abroad just as they can fall ill while in this country

- [ ] Before deciding to dismiss an employee who overstays leave, the employee's age, length of service, reliability record and any explanation given should all be taken into account.

An agreement that an employee should return to work on a particular date will not prevent a complaint of unfair dismissal to an industrial tribunal if an employee is dismissed for failing to return as agreed. In such cases all the factors mentioned above and the need to act reasonably should be borne in mind before any dismissal action is taken.

10

SUB-STANDARD WORK

Key Points:

Careful recruitment, selection and training will minimise the risk of poor performance.

When employment begins, the standards of work required, the consequences of failure to meet them and conditions attaching to any probationary period should be fully explained.

Where warnings are in operation, an employee should be given both time to improve and, where appropriate, training.

The availability of suitable alternative work should be considered before dismissal action is taken.

Any deductions from pay must comply with the provisions of Part II of the Employment Rights Act 1996.

This section considers how to handle problems concerning poor performance and provides guidance on how to encourage improvement.

Setting standards of performance

Employees have a responsibility to achieve a satisfactory level of performance and should be given help and encouragement to reach it. In all cases employers should point out in what way current performance fails to meet the required standard. They should also consider whether any shortfall in performance is due to unreasonable expectations or lack of proper explanation on the part of management. Consideration should be given to whether performance might be improved by suitable training, either internally or from external sources.

Standards of performance provide a means of judging what is acceptable. They should be realistic and measurable in respect of quality, quantity, time and cost. Careful recruitment, selection and training will minimise the risk of poor performance.

The following principles should be observed when employment begins:[15]

☐ The standard of work required should be explained and employees left in no doubt about what is expected of them. Special attention should be paid to ensuring that standards are understood by employees whose English is limited and by young persons with little experience of working life

☐ Where job descriptions are prepared they should accurately convey the main purpose and scope of each job and the tasks involved

☐ Employees should be made aware of the conditions which attach to any probation period

☐ The consequences of any failure to meet the required standards should be explained

☐ Where an employee is promoted, the consequences of failing to make the grade' in the new job should be explained.

What is the role of training and supervision?

Proper training and supervision are essential to the achievement of satisfactory performance. Performance should be discussed regularly with employees, either formally or informally. Steps should be taken to ensure

[15] Further guidance is available in the ACAS Advisory Booklet *Recruitment and Induction*.

10

that inadequate performance, particularly during probation periods, is identified as soon as possible, so that appropriate remedial action can be taken.

Appraisal systems

An appraisal system is a systematic method of obtaining and analysing information to evaluate an employee's performance in a job and assess his or her training and development needs and potential for future promotion. It is essential that appraisal is carried out in a fair and objective manner. Assessment criteria should be non-discriminatory and should be applied irrespective of racial group, sex, marital status or disability. They should be relevant to the requirements of the job. Staff who are responsible for carrying out appraisals should be made aware of the dangers of stereotyping and of making assumptions based on inadequate knowledge.

Negligence or lack of ability

Negligence usually involves a measure of personal blame arising, for example, from lack of motivation or inattention for which some form of disciplinary action will normally be appropriate. Lack of ability, on the other hand, is due to lack of skill or experience and may point to poor recruitment procedures or inadequate training. Where skills have become outmoded by new technology, employers should consider whether new skills could be achieved through training..

How should poor performance be dealt with?

In all cases the cause of poor performance should be investigated. The following guidelines will help to identify the cause and help to ensure that appropriate action is taken:

☐ The employee should be asked for an explanation and the explanation checked or

☐ Where the reason is a lack of the required skills, the employee should, wherever practicable, be assisted through training and given reasonable time to reach the required standard of performance

☐ Where despite encouragement and assistance the employee is unable to reach the required standard of performance, consideration should be given to finding suitable alternative work

10

- [ ] Where alternative work is not available, the position should be explained to the employee before dismissal action is taken

- [ ] An employee should not normally be dismissed because of poor performance unless warnings and a chance to improve have been given

- [ ] if the main cause of poor performance is the changing nature of the job, employers should consider whether the situation may properly be treated as a redundancy matter rather than a capability or conduct issue.[16]

Action in serious cases

Where an employee commits a single error and the actual or potential consequences of that error are extremely serious, warnings will not normally be appropriate. The disciplinary procedure should indicate that dismissal action may be taken in such circumstances.

Dismissal

If employees are unable to achieve a satisfactory level of performance even after an opportunity to improve and with training assistance, the availability of suitable alternative work should be considered. If such work is not available, the situation should be explained sympathetically to the employee before dismissal action is taken.

When are deductions from pay lawful?

Part II of the Employment Rights Act 1996 gives statutory protection against unlawful pay deductions.[17] The Act does not apply to the recovery of an overpayment of wages but it does allow for other deductions from pay in three specified circumstances:

- [ ] Where the deduction is required or authorised by statute; for example, income tax and national insurance deductions; or

- [ ] Where it is required or authorised by 'a relevant provision of the worker's contract'; or

- [ ] Where the worker has signified advance agreement to the deduction in writing.

16 In this context 'redundancy' has a technical meaning defined in Section 139 of the Employment Rights Act 1996. Also see the free booklet *Redundancy Payments* (PL 808) produced by the Department of Trade and Industry.

17 Further guidance is provided in a free booklet produced by the Department of Trade and Industry entitled *Contracts of Employment* (PL 810).

10

The Act also covers the situation where the employer might demand payment of a fine from the worker instead of making a direct deduction. Such a payment must also satisfy one of the conditions outlined above. Deductions made or payments demanded unlawfully cannot be 'legitimised' by later agreement or consent

The Act provides additional protection for those who work in retail employment[18] when the employer makes a deduction or requires payment because of cash shortages or stock deficiencies. Any such deduction is limited to 10 per cent of the gross amount of the wages payable on any pay day (including any deductions due to alleged dishonesty). The employer must, before receiving the first payment for any particular shortage, let the worker know in writing of the full amount owed. Any demand for payment must not be made more than 12 months after the shortage was (or ought reasonably to have been) established. The 10 per cent limit on deductions does not apply to the worker's final payment of wages on termination.

Employers should be aware that there are a number of more effective measures which can be taken to minimise till and stock losses. These include greater care with staff selection, appropriate training, improved supervision and better organisation of the work.

Any worker who thinks an employer has not followed the provisions of the Act has a right to complain to an industrial tribunal. The complaint must normally be presented within three months of the alleged unlawful deduction or payment. Where a tribunal finds a complaint justified, it must order the employer to reimburse the worker accordingly.

Where employment has been terminated, an employee may be able to make a claim for breach of contract to an industrial tribunal for wages or sums of money due under the contract, where the claim 'arises or is outstanding on the termination of employment.' The employer may be able to make a claim against the employee where the employee has claimed against the employer under this legislation.[19]

[18] There is a wide definition given to retail employment. It is employment involving, whether on a regular basis or not, the carrying out of retail transactions or collecting money in respect of the sale or supply of goods or the supply of services (including financial services) directly with the public, fellow workers or other individuals.

[19] Section 3 of the Industrial Tribunals Act 1996.

1

APPENDIX 1

ACAS Code of Practice No. 1

The Employment Protection Act 1975 empowered ACAS to issue Codes of Practice containing such practical guidance as the Service thinks fit for the purpose of promoting the improvement of industrial relations. The Service is required to publish a draft and consider any representations made before transmitting it to the Secretary of State for Employment who shall, if he approves the draft, lay it before Parliament or, if he does not approve it, publish details of his reasons.

NOTE: The footnotes to paragraphs 3 and 4 were amended to take into account the re-enactment provisions of the Employment Protection (Consolidation) Act 1978 and the Employment Act 1989.

Code of Practice 1

Disciplinary practice and procedures in employment

ADVISORY
CONCILIATION
AND
ARBITRATION
SERVICE

This Code from pages one to five is issued pursuant to section 6(1) and (8) of the Employment Protection Act 1975 and comes into effect, by order of the Secretary of State, on 20 June, 1977.

A failure on the part of any person to observe any provision of a Code of Practice shall not of itself render him liable to any proceedings; but in any proceedings before an industrial tribunal or the Central Arbitration Committee any Code of Practice issued under this section shall be admissible in evidence, and if any provision of such a Code appears to the tribunal or Committee to be relevant to any question arising in the proceedings it shall be taken into account in determining that question. (Employment Protection Act 1975 section 6(11).)

Introduction

This Code supersedes paragraphs 130 to 133 (inclusive) of the Code of Practice in effect under Part I of Schedule I to the Trade Union and Labour Relations Act 1974, which paragraphs shall cease to have effect on the date on which this Code comes into effect.

1 This document gives practical guidance on how to draw up disciplinary rules and procedures and how to operate them effectively. Its aim is to help employers and trade unions as well as individual employees—both men and women—wherever they are employed regardless of the size of the organisation in which they work. In the smaller establishments it may not be practicable to adopt all the detailed provisions, but most of the features listed in paragraph 10 could be adopted and incorporated into a simple procedure.

2 ## Why have disciplinary rules and procedures?

Disciplinary rules and procedures are necessary for promoting fairness and order in the treatment of individuals and in the conduct of industrial relations. They also assist an organisation to operate effectively. Rules set standards of conduct at work; procedure helps to ensure that the standards are adhered to and also provides a fair method of dealing with alleged failures to observe them.

3 It is important that employees know what standards of conduct are expected of them and the Contracts of Employment Act 1972 (as amended by the Employment Protection Act 1975) requires employers to provide written information for their employees about certain aspects of their disciplinary rules and procedures.*

4 The importance of disciplinary rules and procedures has also been recognised by the law relating to dismissals, since the grounds for

---

*Section 1 of the Employment Protection (Consolidation) Act 1978 requires employers to provide employees with a written statement of the main terms and conditions of their employment. Section 13 of the Employment Act 1989 amends the Employment Protection (Consolidation) Act 1978 and requires only employers with 20 or more employees to include in such statements any disciplinary rules applicable to employees, and to indicate to whom employees should apply if they are dissatisfied with any disciplinary decisions. The statement should explain any further steps which exist in any procedure for dealing with disciplinary decisions or grievances. The employer may satisfy these requirements by referring the employees to a reasonably accessible document which provides the necessary information. Section 13 is likely to come into force in February 1990. Prior to the 1989 Act all employers were required to include a note on discipline, regardless of the number of employed.

dismissal and the way in which the dismissal has been handled can be challenged before an industrial tribunal.* Where either of these is found by a tribunal to have been unfair the employer may be ordered to reinstate or re-engage the employees concerned and may be liable to pay compensation to them.

Formulating policy

5 Management is responsible for maintaining discipline within the organisation and for ensuring that there are adequate disciplinary rules and procedures. The initiative for establishing these will normally lie with management. However, if they are to be fully effective the rules and procedures need to be accepted as reasonable both by those who are to be covered by them and by those who operate them. Management should therefore aim to secure the involvement of employees and all levels of management when formulating new or revising existing rules and procedures. In the light of particular circumstances in different companies and industries trade union officials** may or may not wish to participate in the formulation of the rules but they should participate fully with management in agreeing the procedural arrangements which will apply to their members and in seeing that these arrangements are used consistently and fairly.

Rules

6 It is unlikely that any set of disciplinary rules can cover all circumstances that may arise : moreover the rules required will vary according to particular circumstances such as the type of work, working conditions and size of establishment. When drawing up rules the aim should be to specify clearly and concisely those necessary for the efficient and safe performance of work and for the maintenance of satisfactory relations within the workforce and between employees and management. Rules should not be so general as to be meaningless.

7 Rules should be readily available and management should make every effort to ensure that employees know and understand them. This may be best achieved by giving every employee a copy of the rules and by

*Section 67 (2) of the Employment (Consolidation) Act 1978 specifies that a complaint of unfair dismissal has to be presented to an Industrial Tribunal before the end of the 3-month period beginning with the effective date of termination.

**Throughout this Code, trade union official has the meaning assigned to it by S.30 (1) of the Trade Union and Labour Relations Act 1974 and means, broadly, officers of the union, its branches and sections, and anyone else, including fellow employees, appointed or elected under the union's rules to represent members.

explaining them orally. In the case of new employees this should form part of an induction programme.

8 Employees should be made aware of the likely consequences of breaking rules and in particular they should be given a clear indication of the type of conduct which may warrant summary dismissal.

Essential features of disciplinary procedures

9 Disciplinary procedures should not be viewed primarily as a means of imposing sanctions. They should also be designed to emphasise and encourage improvements in individual conduct.

10 Disciplinary procedures should:
(a) Be in writing.
(b) Specify to whom they apply.
(c) Provide for matters to be dealt with quickly.
(d) Indicate the disciplinary actions which may be taken.
(e) Specify the levels of management which have the authority to take the various forms of disciplinary action, ensuring that immediate superiors do not normally have the power to dismiss without reference to senior management.
(f) Provide for individuals to be informed of the complaints against them and to be given an opportunity to state their case before decisions are reached.
(g) Give individuals the right to be accompanied by a trade union representative or by a fellow employee of their choice.
(h) Ensure that, except for gross misconduct, no employees are dismissed for a first breach of discipline.
(i) Ensure that disciplinary action is not taken until the case has been carefully investigated.
(j) Ensure that individuals are given an explanation for any penalty imposed.
(k) Provide a right of appeal and specify the procedure to be followed.

The procedure in operation

11 When a disciplinary matter arises, the supervisor or manager should first establish the facts promptly before recollections fade, taking into account the statements of any available witnesses. In serious cases consideration should be given to a brief period of suspension while the case is investigated and this suspension should be with pay. Before a decision is made or penalty imposed the individual should be interviewed and given the opportunity to state his or her case and should be advised of any rights under the procedure, including the right to be accompanied.

3

12 Often supervisors will give informal oral warnings for the purpose of improving conduct when employees commit minor infringements of the established standards of conduct. However, where the facts of a case appear to call for disciplinary action, other than summary dismissal, the following procedure should normally be observed :

(a) In the case of minor offences the individual should be given a formal oral warning or if the issue is more serious, there should be a written warning setting out the nature of the offence and the likely consequences of further offences. In either case the individual should be advised that the warning constitutes the first formal stage of the procedure.

(b) Further misconduct might warrant a final written warning which should contain a statement that any recurrence would lead to suspension or dismissal or some other penalty, as the case may be.

(c) The final step might be disciplinary transfer, or disciplinary suspension without pay (but only if these are allowed for by an express or implied condition of the contract of employment), or dismissal, according to the nature of the misconduct. Special consideration should be given before imposing disciplinary suspension without pay and it should not normally be for a prolonged period.

13 Except in the event of an oral warning, details of any disciplinary action should be given in writing to the employee and if desired, to his or her representative. At the same time the employee should be told of any right of appeal, how to make it and to whom.

14 When determining the disciplinary action to be taken the supervisor or manager should bear in mind the need to satisfy the test of reasonableness in all the circumstances, So far as possible, account should be taken of the employee's record and any other relevant factors.

15 Special consideration should be given to the way in which disciplinary procedures are to operate in exceptional cases. For example :

(a) **Employees to whom the full procedure is not immediately available.** Special provisions may have to be made for the handling of disciplinary matters among nightshift workers, workers in isolated locations or depots or others who may pose particular problems for example because no one is present with the necessary authority to take disciplinary action or no trade union representative is immediately available.

(b) **Trade union officials.** Disciplinary action against a trade union official can lead to a serious dispute if it is seen as an attack on the union's functions. Although normal disciplinary standards should apply to their conduct as employees, no disciplinary action beyond

4

an oral warning should be taken until the circumstances of the case have been discussed with a senior trade union representative or full-time official.

(c) **Criminal offences outside employment.** These should not be treated as automatic reasons for dismissal regardless of whether the offence has any relevance to the duties of the individual as an employee. The main considerations should be whether the offence is one that makes the individual unsuitable for his or her type of work or unacceptable to other employees. Employees should not be dismissed solely because a charge against them is pending or because they are absent through having been remanded in custody.

Appeals

16 Grievance procedures are sometimes used for dealing with disciplinary appeals though it is normally more appropriate to keep the two kinds of procedure separate since the disciplinary issues are in general best resolved within the organisation and need to be dealt with more speedily than others. The external stages of a grievance procedure may however, be the appropriate machinery for dealing with appeals against disciplinary action where a final decision within the organisation is contested or where the matter becomes a collective issue between management and a trade union.

17 Independent arbitration is sometimes an appropriate means of resolving disciplinary issues. Where the parties concerned agree, it may constitute the final stage of procedure.

Records

18 Records should be kept, detailing the nature of any breach of disciplinary rules the action taken and the reasons for it, whether an appeal was lodged, its outcome and any subsequent developments. These records should be carefully safeguarded and kept confidential.

19 Except in agreed special circumstances breaches of disciplinary rules should be disregarded after a specified period of satisfactory conduct.

Further action

20 Rules and procedures should be reviewed periodically in the light of any developments in employment legislation or industrial relations practice and, if necessary, revised in order to ensure their continuing relevance and effectiveness. Any amendments and additional rules imposing new obligations should be introduced only after reasonable notice has been given to all employees and, where appropriate, their representatives have been informed.

5

2

APPENDIX 2

Rules for small companies

As a minimum rules should:

- [ ] Be simple, clear and in writing
- [ ] Be displayed prominently in the workplace
- [ ] Be known and fully understood by all employees
- [ ] Cover issues such as absence, timekeeping, health and safety and use of company facilities (Add others relevant to your organisation).
- [ ] Indicate the type of conduct which will normally lead to disciplinary action other than dismissal – examples may include persistent lateness or unauthorised absence
- [ ] Indicate the type of conduct which will normally lead to dismissal without notice – examples may include working dangerously, stealing or fighting – although much will depend on the circumstances of each offence.

3

APPENDIX 3

Example 1 (any organisation)

DISCIPLINARY PROCEDURE

(1) Purpose and scope

This procedure is designed to help and encourage all employees to achieve and maintain standards of conduct, attendance and job performance. The company rules (a copy of which is displayed in the office) and this procedure apply to all employees. The aim is to ensure consistent and fair treatment for all.

(2) Principles

a) No disciplinary action will be taken against an employee until the case has been fully investigated.

b) At every stage in the procedure the employee will be advised of the nature of the complaint against him or her and will be given the opportunity to state his or her case before any decision is made.

c) At all stages the employee will have the right to be accompanied by a shop steward, employee representative or work colleague during the disciplinary interview.

d) No employee will be dismissed for a first breach of discipline except in the case of gross misconduct when the penalty will be dismissal without notice or payment in lieu of notice.

e) An employee will have the right to appeal against any disciplinary penalty imposed.

f) The procedure may be implemented at any stage if the employee's alleged misconduct warrants such action.

(3) The Procedure

Minor faults will be dealt with informally but where the matter is more serious the following procedure will be used:

Stage 1 – Oral warning

If conduct or performance does not meet acceptable standards the employee will normally be given a formal ORAL WARNING. He or she will be advised of the reason for the warning, that it is the first stage of the disciplinary procedure and of his or her right of appeal. A brief note of the oral warning will be kept but it will be spent after..... months, subject to satisfactory conduct and performance.

Stage 2 – Written warning

If the offence is a serious one, or if a further offence occurs, a WRITTEN WARNING will be given to the employee by the supervisor. This will give details of the complaint, the improvement required and the timescale. It will warn that action under Stage 3 will be considered if there is no satisfactory improvement and will advise of the right of appeal. A copy of this written warning will be kept by the supervisor but it will be disregarded for disciplinary purposes after..... months subject to satisfactory conduct and performance.

Stage 3 – Final written warning or disciplinary suspension

If there is still a failure to improve and conduct or performance is still unsatisfactory, or if the misconduct is sufficiently serious to warrant only one written warning but insufficiently serious to justify dismissal (in effect both first and final written warning), a FINAL WRITTEN WARNING will normally be given to the employee. This will give details of the complaint, will warn that dismissal will result if there is no satisfactory improvement and will advise of the right of appeal. A copy of this final written warning will be kept by the supervisor but it will be spent after ...

months (in exceptional cases the period may be longer) subject to satisfactory conduct and performance.

Alternatively, consideration will be given to imposing a penalty of a disciplinary suspension without pay for up to a maximum of five working days.

Stage 4 – Dismissal

If conduct or performance is still unsatisfactory and the employee still fails to reach the prescribed standards, DISMISSAL will normally result. Only the appropriate Senior Manager can take the decision to dismiss. The employee will be provided, as soon as reasonably practicable, with written reasons for dismissal, the date on which employment will terminate and the right of appeal.

(4) Gross Misconduct

The following list provides examples of offences which are normally regarded as gross misconduct:

theft, fraud, deliberate falsification of records

fighting, assault on another person

deliberate damage to company property

serious incapability through alcohol or being under the influence of illegal drugs

serious negligence which causes unacceptable loss, damage or injury

serious act of insubordination

unauthorised entry to computer records.

If you are accused of an act of gross misconduct, you may be suspended from work on full pay, normally for no more than five working days, while the company investigates the alleged offence. If, on completion of the investigation and the full disciplinary procedure, the company is satisfied that gross misconduct has occurred, the result will normally be summary dismissal without notice or payment in lieu of notice.

(5) Appeals

An employee who wishes to appeal against a disciplinary decision should inform .... within two working days. The Senior Manager will hear all appeals and his/her decision is final. At the appeal any disciplinary penalty imposed will be reviewed but it cannot be increased.

Example 2 (small firms)
DISCIPLINARY PROCEDURE
(1) Purpose and scope
The Company's aim is to encourage improvement in individual conduct. This procedure sets out the action which will be taken when disciplinary rules are breached.

(2) Principles
a) The procedure is designed to establish the facts quickly and to deal consistently with disciplinary issues. No disciplinary action will be taken until the matter has been fully investigated.
b) At every stage employees will have the opportunity to state their case and be represented, if they wish, at the hearings by a shop steward if appropriate, or by a fellow employee.
c) An employee has the right to appeal against any disciplinary penalty.

(3) The Procedure
Stage 1 – Oral warning
If conduct or performance is unsatisfactory, the employee will be given a formal **ORAL WARNING**, which will be recorded. The warning will be disregarded after . . . . months satisfactory service.

Stage 2 – Written warning
If the offence is serious, if there is no improvement in standards, or if a further offence occurs, a **WRITTEN WARNING** will be given which will include the reason for the warning and a note that, if there is no improvement after . . . . months, a FINAL WRITTEN WARNING will be given.

Stage 3 – Final written warning
If conduct or performance is still unsatisfactory, **A FINAL WRITTEN WARNING** will be given making it

clear that any recurrence of the offence or other serious misconduct within a period of . . . . months will result in dismissal.

Stage 4 – Dismissal

If there is no satisfactory improvement or if further serious misconduct occurs, the employee will be DISMISSED.

Gross misconduct

If, after investigation, it is confirmed that an employee has committed an offence of the following nature (the list is not exhaustive), the normal consequence will be dismissal:

theft, damage to company property, fraud, incapacity for work due to being under the influence of alcohol or illegal drugs, physical assault and gross insubordination.

While the alleged gross misconduct is being investigated the employee may be suspended, during which time he or she will be paid the normal hourly rate. Any decision to dismiss will be taken by the employer only after a full investigation.

(5) Appeals

An employee who wishes to appeal against any disciplinary decision must do so to the employer within two working days. The employer will hear the appeal and decide the case as impartially as possible.

4

APPENDIX 4

Example letters

(i) Notice of Disciplinary interview

Dear ....

Date ....

I am writing to tell you that you are required to attend a disciplinary interview on .... at .... am/pm which is to be held in .... At this interview the question of disciplinary action against you, in accordance with the Company's disciplinary procedure, will be considered with regard to:

You are entitled, if you wish, to be accompanied by another work colleague or your trade union representative.

Signed..........

Manager

(ii) Notice of written warning or final written warning*

Dear ....

Date ....

You attended a disciplinary interview on .... I am writing to confirm the decision taken that you be given a written warning/final written warning* under the second/third* stage of the Company Disciplinary Procedure.

This warning will be placed in your personal file but will be disregarded for disciplinary purposes after a period of ....months provided your conduct** improves/performance reaches a satisfactory level.

a)   The nature of the unsatisfactory conduct or performance was:

b)   The conduct or performance improvement expected is:

c)   The timescale within which the improvement is required is:

d)   The likely consequence of further misconduct or insufficient improvement is:

Final written warning/dismissal*

You have the right of appeal against this decision (in writing**) to.......... within .... days of receiving this disciplinary warning.

Yours sincerely

Manager

Note: * The wording should be amended as appropriate
      ** Delete if inappropriate

(iii) Confirmation of dismissal (following previous warnings)

Dear ....

Date.................

On .... you were informed in writing that you would be given a final written warning in accordance with Stage .... of the Company Disciplinary Procedure. In that letter you were warned that if your conduct/performance* did not improve, you were likely to be dismissed.

At the disciplinary hearing held on .... it was decided that your conduct/performance* was still unsatisfactory and that you be dismissed.

I am therefore writing to you to confirm the decision that you be dismissed in accordance with Stage .... of the Company Disciplinary Procedure and that your last day of service with the Company will be .... The reasons for your dismissal are:

You have the right of appeal against this decision (in writing**) to .... within................ days of receiving this notice of dismissal.

Yours sincerely

Manager

Note: *The wording should be amended as appropriate

**Delete if inappropriate

(iv) Confirmation of dismissal (without previous warnings)

4

Dear ....

Date...............

I am writing to confirm the decision taken at the disciplinary hearing held on .... that you be summarily dismissed without notice or payment in lieu of notice, in accordance with the Company Disciplinary Procedure. Your last day of service was...............

The reasons for your dismissal are:

You have the right of appeal against this decision (in writing*) to .... within .... days of receiving this notice of dismissal.

Yours sincerely

Manager

Note: *The wording should be amended as appropriate

Dear ....

Date................

You have appealed against the oral warning/written warning/final written warning/notice of dismissal* confirmed to you in writing on .... Your appeal will be heard by.............. on.............. at
....

The decision of this appeal hearing is final and there is no further right of review.

You have the right to appear alone or to be accompanied by your Trade Union/Staff Organisation representative or a fellow employee.

Yours sincerely

Manager

Note: *The wording should be amended as appropriate.

(v) Notice of appeal hearing

(vi) Notice of result of appeal hearing

Dear ....

Date.....................

You appealed against the decision of the disciplinary hearing that you be given a .... warning/be dismissed* in accordance with Stage ... of the Company Disciplinary Procedure. The appeal hearing was held on ....

I am now writing to confirm the decision taken by the Manager who conducted the appeal hearing, namely that the decision to .... stands*/the decision to .... be revoked* (specify if no disciplinary action is being taken or what the new disciplinary action is).

You have now exercised your right of appeal under the Company Disciplinary Procedure and this decision is final.

Yours sincerely

Manager

Note   The wording should be amended as appropriate.

*Delete if inappropriate

(vii) Model letter of enquiry regarding likely cause of absence addressed to an employee's general practitioner

Doctor's name ....
Address ....
....

Date....................................
....

PLEASE ACKNOWLEDGE RECEIPT OF
THIS LETTER IF THERE IS LIKELY
TO BE ANY DELAY IN REPLYING

Re:
Name ....
Address ....

To administer Statutory Sick Pay, and the Company's sick pay scheme, and to plan the work in the department, it would be helpful to have a report on your patient, who is our employee.

His/her work as a...................................... has the following major features:

    Management responsibility for ....
    Seated/standing/mobile
    Light/medium/heavy effort required
    Day/shift/night work
    Clerical/secretarial duties
    Group I (private)/Group II (professional) driver
    Other ....

The absence record for the past year is summarised as:

    Total days lost ....
    This month ....
    Previous months ....

Attached is your patient's permission to enquire — He/she wishes/does not wish to have access to the report under the Access to Medical Reports Act 1988:

    What is the likely date of return to work?
    Will there be any disability at that time?
    How long is it likely to last?
    Are there any reasonable adjustments we could make to accommodate the disability?
    Is there any underlying medical reason for this attendance record?
    Is he/she likely to be able to render regular and efficient service in the future?

Is there any specific recommendation you wish to make about him/her which would help in finding him/her an alternative job, if that is necessary, and if there is an opportunity for redeployment (eg: no climbing ladders, no driving, etc).

I would be grateful for an early reply and enclose a stamped addressed envelope.

Please attach your account to the report (following the BMA guidance on fees).

Yours sincerely

Signed ....

Name ....
(BLOCK LETTERS)
Role in the
company ....

Please amend/delete where necessary

(If one is available, it may be helpful to send a copy of the employee's job description)

Publications

The role of ACAS
Preventing and resolving industrial disputes
Providing information and advice
Individual employment rights
Appeals procedures for individual employees: the role of third parties

Advisory Handbooks
Employing people: a handbook for small firms
Discipline at work
Employment handbook

Advisory Booklets
Job evaluation: an introduction
Introduction to payment systems
Personnel records
Absence and labour turnover
Recruitment and induction
Employee communications and consultation
The company handbook
Employment policies
Employee appraisal
Redundancy handling
Hours of work
Appraisal-related pay
Health and employment
Effective organisations: the people factor
Supervision
Recruitment policies for the 1990s
Teamwork: success through people

Occasional Papers
51 Motivating and rewarding employees: some aspects of theory and practice
52 Time for a change: forging labour-management partnerships
53 A change of culture
54 Teamwork: key issues and developments
55 Joint problem solving: does it work? An evaluation of ACAS in-depth advisory mediation
56 Asking ACAS: an evaluation of the ACAS public enquiry point service

Codes of Practice
1 Disciplinary practice and procedures in employment
2 Disclosure of information to trade unions for collective bargaining purposes
3 Time off for trade union duties and activities
(Codes of Practice are available only from HMSO)

Reading Lists
3 Absence
5 Team working
10 Flexible working patterns
19 Conflict resolution
38 Job satisfaction
39 Quality of working life
46 Performance appraisal
53 Organisational culture

For details of how to order ACAS Publications, please write to:
ACAS Reader Ltd, PO Box 16, Earl Shilton, Leicester LE9 8ZZ
or telephone: 01455 852225.
For all other enquiries, see list of regional ACAS addresses on p72.

ACAS Public Enquiry Points

Birmingham	Tel: (0121) 622 5050
Bristol	Tel: (0117) 974 4066
Cardiff	Tel: (01222) 761126
Fleet	Tel: (01252) 811868
Glasgow	Tel: (0141) 204 2677
Leeds	Tel: (0113) 243 1371
Liverpool	Tel: (0151) 427 8881
London	Tel: (0171) 396 5100
Manchester	Tel: (0161) 228 3222
Newcastle upon Tyne	Tel: (0191) 261 2191
Nottingham	Tel: (0115) 969 3355

ACAS main offices

Midlands Region
Leonard House, 319/323 Bradford Street, Birmingham B5 6ET

Anderson House, Clinton Avenue, Nottingham NG5 1AW

Northern Region
Commerce House, St Alban's Place, Leeds LS2 8HH

Westgate House, Westgate Road, Newcastle upon Tyne NE1 1TJ

North West Region
Boulton House, 17-21 Chorlton Street, Manchester M1 3HY

Cressington House, 249 St Mary's Road, Garston, Liverpool L19 0NF

South and West Region
Regent House, 27a Regent Street, Clifton, Bristol BS8 4HR

Westminster House, Fleet Road, Fleet, Hants GU13 8PD

London, Eastern and Southern Areas
Clifton House, 83-117 Euston Road, London NW1 2RB

39 King Street, Thetford, Norfolk IP24 1AU

Suites 3-5, Business Centre, 1-7 Commercial Road, Paddock Wood, Kent TN12 6EN

Scotland
Franborough House, 123-157 Bothwell Street, Glasgow G2 7JR

Wales
3 Purbeck House, Lambourne Crescent, Llanishen, Cardiff CF4 5GJ

Head Office
Brandon House, 180 Borough High Street, London SE1 1LW

Printed in England by Flair Press Ltd
20th impression 3/97 (INF/P/7/88b)